KiDS'
JOKES

KiDS' JOKES

Capella

This edition published in 2008 by Arcturus Publishing Limited
26/27 Bickels Yard, 151–153 Bermondsey Street,
London SE1 3HA

Copyright © 2008 Arcturus Publishing Limited

ISBN: 978-1-84837-071-5

Illustrations by Peter Coupe

Printed in China

Contents

Nutty Names...

What do you call a man who does everything at top speed?

Max!

What do you call a man with a cable
coming out of his ear ?

Mike !

What do you call a woman with a sinking ship on
her head ?

Mandy Lifeboats !

What do you call a man who fills himself
with fried slices of potato and makes a
noise in the cinema ?

Chris Packet !

What do you call a super hero who
looks after books ?

Conan the Librarian !

What do you call an overweight vampire ?

Draculard !

What do you call a woman who works
for a solicitor ?

Sue !

What do you call a man who goes fishing
every weekend ?

Rod !

What do you call a teacher
with earplugs in ?

**Anything you like - he can't
hear you !**

What do you call a failed lion tamer ?

Claude Bottom !

What do you call twin brothers with drums on
their heads ?

Tom, Tom !

What do you call a man and woman who show you up in front of your friends ?

Mum and Dad !

What do you call a man who likes drawing and painting ?

Art !

What do you call a man who does odd jobs and lives just round the corner ?

Andy !

Prisoner - It's not my fault. I was given a name that was bound to lead me into crime !

Judge - What is your name ?

Prisoner - Robin Banks !

What do you call a woman who hates butter ?

Marge !

What do you call a 35 stone sumo wrestler ?

Whatever he tells you to !

What's the name of a really strict female teacher ?

Miss Laura Norder !

What do you call a man who corrects examination papers ?

Mark !

What do you call a man with seagull on his head ?

Cliff !

What do you call a woman who only goes out at Christmas ?

Carol !

What do you call a masked man who lends you money ?

The Loan Arranger !

What do you call a woman who checks punctuation ?

Dot !

I call him Bill - he's always asking me for money !

What do you call the man who used to make his living selling refreshments in the interval at football matches ?

Alf Time !

What do you call a
Scotsman with his own
computer ?

Mac !

What do you call a woman
who can makes pints
disappear in a pub ?

Beatrix !

What do you call a man who keeps pet rabbits ?

Warren !

What do you call a man who
keeps pet rabbits and
writes epic novels ?

Warren Peace !

What do you call a man who
keeps an angry ferret down
his pants ?

Very, very stupid !

What do you call the man who stamps the letters at the Post Office ?

Frank !

What do you call a man who works in a perfume shop at Christmas ?

Frank in Scents !

What do you call a woman having a meal in a restaurant ?

Anita !

What do you call a Spanish woman having a meal in a restaurant ?

Juanita !

If you were called Jack you could lift my car and mend the puncture at the back !

What do you call a girl who has her own car ?

Minnie !

★

Is it true that the man who invented the toilet
was called Lou ?

★

What do you call someone with more
money than sense ?

My best friend !

★

The dimmest boy in my class has the same initials
as the contents of his head.....M.T.

★

What do you call a woman
who has a boat tied up at
the riverside ?

Maude !

What do you call a man with loads of money ?

Rich !

What do you call a fish that
services pianos ?

A piano tuna !

What do you call Mr Smith's half brother ?

Arthur Smith !

What do you call a
magician's assistant ?

Trixie !

What do you call someone
who never blows his nose ?

Ronnie !

What do you call a man who likes to grow flowers, fruit and vegetables?

Gordon!

★

What do you call the brother and sister who like to build things across rivers?

Archie and Bridget!

★

What do you call a girl who likes to cook in the garden?

Barbie!

★

What do you call a woman with a food processor on her head?

Belinda!

★

Who was the first man to do math?

Adam!

What do you call a man who hosts a quiz show
at Christmas ?

Santa Clues !

What do you call someone who claps when
contestants get the right answer ?

Santapplause !

What do you call a man who doesn't sink ?

Bob !

What do you call a man who lies in front of your
door all day ?

Matt !

What do you call a girl with lots of suitcases ?

Carrie !

★

What do you call cattle thieves who wear tissue paper trousers ?

Rustlers !

★

That frog is a secret agent - his name's Pond...

...James Pond !

★

What do you call a man who slowly runs out of energy ?

Peter !

★

What do you call a girl who never stands up straight ?

Eileen !

What do you call
a girl who lives in
a pond ?

Lily !

★

What do you call
a nun with a
radio on her
head ?

A transister !

★

What do you call
a teacher who
eats toffees in
class ?

A chew-tor !

★

What do you call someone who carries a soccer
team from one match to another ?

The coach !

What do you call someone that witches go to when they are sick ?

A witch doctor, of course !

What do you call an Eskimo's house if it doesn't have a toilet ?

An ig !

What do you call a house in France with two toilets ?

WELCOME TO
TOULOUSE

1 2

Toulouse !

What do you call it when a toilet is closed and bricked up ?

Loo - brick - ation !

What do you call the gap in a play for going to the toilet ?

The inter - lood !

What do you call a teacher who has a
lot of accidents ?

Miss Hap !

What do you call the hairstyle you get from
sticking your head in an oven ?

A micro - wave !

What was the name of the explorer with a
passion for biscuits ?

Captain Cookie !

What do you call the boy who is also a goat ?

Billy !

What do you call the woman who brings him to
school every day ?

His nanny !

School
Screams

Teacher – You should have been here at
9 o'clock this morning !

Pupil – Why, did something happen ?

Teacher - Who can tell me where Hadrian's Wall is ?

Pupil - Around Hadrian's garden, Miss !

★

My last school was so bad they didn't have a school photograph - they sent home identikit pictures instead !

Science teacher - Gary, do you know what Copper Nitrate is ?

Gary - Yes Sir it's what they pay policemen on night duty !

★

Teacher - Now come on Martin, where do you think I would find Hadrian's wall ?

Martin - Wherever Hadrian left it, Sir !

★

Math teacher - Carol, why have you brought a picture of Henry the Eighth in with you ?

Carol - You told us to bring a ruler in with us today !

Teacher - name one of Noah's children !

Pupil - Joan of Arc ?

For all those who were late this morning because they stayed up to watch the football, we're going to make school more like football...

you will all stay behind and do extra time tonight as a penalty !

Math teacher - Blenkinsop, can you tell me the 9 times table please ?

Blenkinsop - You asked me that yesterday, don't tell me you've forgotten it already !

Teacher - You're on English level 4 aren't you, Smith ?

Smith - Yes.

Teacher - Then take this English level 2 book for your father or he's never going to be able to catch up and do your homework properly !

Of course in my day you only had the one choice
for school dinners...

...Like it or lump it !

★

Where do Martians go to train to be
teachers ?

Mooniversity !

★

I think my math
teacher is in love
with me...

How do you work that
out ?

...she puts red kisses all
over my homework !

★

What's the best snake
to take into a math
lesson ?

An adder !

I would have done my homework, but...

I didn't have any pocket money left and my sister always demands cash in advance...

My dad was working late and he has all the brains in the family...

My pen ran out and I spent all night looking for an inkwell...

What is a history teacher's favourite fruit ?

A date !

Please Miss, is it true that the French only ever eat one egg for breakfast ?

What makes you ask that ?

Because yesterday you said that in France, one egg is un oeuf !

Did you hear about the teacher who had to wear sunglasses in the classroom ?

He had extremely bright pupils !

Anxious parent - What do you think my son will be when he has finished all his exams ?

Teacher - A very old man !

How many teachers does it take to work the photocopier ?

Who cares, as long as it keeps them out of the classroom !

Head - You boy, stop running around like that ! Don't you know who I am ?

Pupil - There's a bloke here who doesn't even know who he is !

Why do swimming teachers like elephants ?

Because they never forget their trunks !

We've got a new drama teacher -
she's a real class act !

Head - That's Hodgkiss, the school bully.

Visitor - How dreadful, can't you do anything to stop him ?

Head - Certainly not, or I'd never get the teachers back to the classrooms after lunch break !

Who is a teacher's favourite actor ?

Michael Caine !

Eric should make an excellent train driver as he has more experience of lines than any other pupil in the school !

Our cookery teacher knows his onions...

Our P.E. teacher thinks we're a real shower...

Our last math teacher was taken away...

Our music teacher never accepts notes
from home...

Where do new teachers come from ?

They're produced on an assembly line !

What were the names of
the very first teachers ?

Miss and Sir !

Teacher - Is your father helping you with your
homework ?

Pupil - No Sir, if anything he knows even less than
I do !

Well, son, how did you find the math exam ?

Unfortunately, it wasn't lost !

Teacher - Smith, give me a sentence with the word 'politics' in it.

Smith - My pet parrot swallowed the alarm clock and now Polly ticks !

What's the best way to tell your math teacher that you have forgotten to do your homework - again ?

From a great distance !

Teacher - If your father gave you $1.50 pocket money and your mother gave you $2.50, what would you have ?

Pupil - Someone else's parents !

Pupil - Do I need any qualifications to work as a Father Christmas in a department store ?

Careers teacher - You need Ho ! Ho ! Ho ! levels !

Teacher - Well, at least I know that no-one in the school football team will ever start smoking.

Head - How do you work that out ?

Teacher - Because they always lose their matches !

Our school cook was arrested for cruelty - she was caught beating eggs, battering fish and whipping cream !

John - I bet our chemistry teacher could cure your insomnia, Mum...

Mum - Why, is he a doctor as well ?

John - No, but as soon as he starts to speak half the class falls asleep !

Teacher - Are you sending Gary to boarding school ?

Parent - Yes. His report says he is always bored !

Games teacher - Read these books and they will help you get fit - they're exercise books !

We're going to build a bonfire, put our math books on the top, put school dinners in the middle, and burn the bloomin' lot !

Teacher - How many letters are in the alphabet ?

Pupil - 25 !

Teacher - How did you work that out ?

Pupil - Well, it's Christmas next week, so there's Noel !

Head - Why did you call alien investigators into the school?

Pupil - I looked into the school kitchen and saw an unidentified frying object !

Teacher -Jenkins, what's the difference between an elephant and *my* desk ?

Jenkins - Don't know sir.

Teacher - In that case I think I'll send someone else to put these books in *my* desk drawers !

Teacher - I just don't understand how one person can make so many mistakes in their homework !

Pupil - Oh I can't take all the credit, Sir, my dad did most of it !

We sent our teacher's photograph to a lonely hearts' club...

They sent it straight back - they said they weren't THAT lonely !

How can you tell when a teacher is in a good mood ?

Don't ask me !

What do you call a teacher with a pile of sports equipment on his head ?

Jim !

What do you call a man with a school on his head ?

Ed !

What do math teachers do when their sinks get blocked ?

They work it out with a pencil !

What do cannibals have for school dinners ?

Snake and pygmy pie, with chimps and beings !

What do you call a boy who only just gets to school on time every day ?

Justin !

Did you hear about the math teacher who wanted an Italian take away, but was divided about whether to have additional cheese ?

Our technology teacher left to try and make something of himself !

Who's your favourite teacher ?

The Finnish one !

We haven't got any Finnish teachers !

Yes we have. Every day she says "Finish what you're doing and go home !"

Teacher - You copies from Fred's exam paper didn't you?

Pupil - How did you know?

Teacher - Fred's paper says "I don't know" and you have put "Me neither"!

Steve - I wish MY dad would help me with my homework like yours does !

Joe - I wish your dad would help me as well. I got 3 out of 25 and another detention thanks to mine !

Animal
Antics

Looks like reindeer !

What do you call a goat who robs banks ?

Billy the Kid !

What should you name a bald teddy?

Fred bear!

If a house mouse sleeps in a house
and a field mouse sleeps in a field
do dormice sleep in dorms ?

Where do rabbits go when they want something
to read ?

Buck shops !

Rabbit - How do I know this TV will work when I
get it home ?

Shopkeeper - It comes with a full warrenty !

How do lovebirds dance ?

Chick to chick !

Why do elephants paint
their toenails red ?

**So they can hide in
cherry trees !**

If a rooster lays an egg on the middle of a slanted
roof, on which side will it fall ?

Neither side. Roosters don't lay eggs !

Why is the sky so high ?

So birds don't bump their heads !

What says 'Now you see me, now you don't ?'

A zebra using a pelican crossing !

What do you get if you sit under a cow ?

A pat on the head !

Why do seagulls live near the sea?

Because if they lived near the bay, they would be called bagels !

What do porcupines eat with their cheese ?

Prickled onions !

What do you get if you cross a cow with a camel ?

Lumpy custard !

How do you stop rabbits digging up your garden ?

Easy - take their spades away !

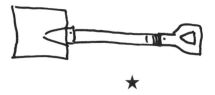

Why did the turkey cross the road ?

To prove he wasn't chicken !

We call our dog
Blacksmith because
every now and again
he makes
a bolt for the door !

Why are you taking that snake
into the math exam ?

It's an adder !

What fish only swims at night ?

The starfish !

What did the buffalo say to his little boy when he
left on a school trip?

Bison !

★

How do you fit more pigs onto a farm ?

Build a sty - scraper !

What is a rabbit's favourite kind of music ?

Hip-hop !

What goes 'Mark, Mark...'

A dog with a swollen lip !

What are baby crabs called ?

Nippers !

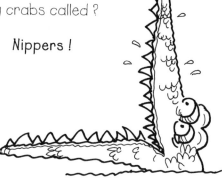

Waiter! Bring me a crocodile sandwich...
and make it snappy !

Did you hear about the pony who
was asked to leave the animal choir ?

She was always a little horse !

Police are looking for a criminal octopus...

He is well armed and dangerous !

What lies at the bottom of the sea and shivers ?

A nervous wreck !

What is the fastest fish in the lake ?

A motor pike !

What does a cat like to eat for breakfast ?

Mice Crispies !

Did you know that alligators eat beans for breakfast ?

Human beans of course !

Noah's Ark was able to find its way about at night because it had been fitted with floodlights !

Why do bees hum ?

Because they have forgotten the words !

Where do you take an injured bee ?

To the waspital !

...but you would take an injured pony to the horsepital !

★

Why do railway porters like elephants ?

Because they always carry their own trunks !

What has 10 legs, 3 heads but only 2 arms ?

A man and a dog sitting on a zebra !

What's grey and zooms through the jungle at 70 miles an hour ?

An elephant on a motorbike !

Why should you never play cards in the jungle ?

Because there are too many cheetahs about !

What vegetable do you get if you cross a sheepdog with a bunch of daffodils ?

A collie - flower !

What bird lights up the farmyard at night ?

A battery hen !

What game do horses play ?

Stable tennis !

Why did the hedgehog cross the road ?

He wanted to see his flat mate !

Why did the dinosaur cross the road ?

Because chickens hadn't been invented
in those days !

Why did the cat cross the road ?

To see his friend who worked in the
chemists - Puss in Boots !

Why did the snake
cross the road ?

Because it couldn't
use the footbridge !

How do rabbits travel?

By hareplane !

Why did the duck cross the road ?

It was the chicken's day off !

What do schools of mackerel do before an exam ?

Re - fish - ion !

Why do elephants have wrinkles ?

Because they hate ironing !

How do you know if an elephant has been in your fridge ?

They leave footprints in the butter !

What creature comes in handy on a car ?

A windscreen viper !

Why didn't the young cat get into trouble for telling lies ?

He was only kitten !

What is yellow and very dangerous ?

Shark infested custard !

What does it mean if you find a set of horse shoes ?

Some poor horse is walking around in his socks !

Where do rabbits go for an eye test ?

To the hoptician !

What happens when it rains cats and dogs ?

You can step in a poodle !

What's another name for parrot food ?

Pollyfilla !

Did you hear about the dog who was too lazy to dig up his bone ?

He was bone idle !

How many sheep does it take to make a sweater ?

I didn't even know that sheep could knit !

Who stole the soap ?

The robber ducky !

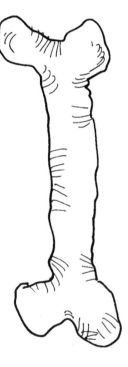

Why does a giraffe have such a long neck ?

Have you ever smelled a giraffe's feet ?

Bullfighting
for
beginners

by

Matt A. Dores

When sheep are cold they gather in a big circle
and a few sheep in the centre make a lot of
noise and this keeps everyone else warm...

...it's called central bleating !

What do the police have to have before they can
come into your home looking for parrots ?

A perch warrant !

What do you call a sheep with a machine gun ?

Lambo !

What does a cat rest his head on in bed ?

A caterpiller !

What sort of cat sells wood ?

A cat - a - log !

What part of a car can be used to change cats into something else ?

The cat - alytic converter !

What bulls hide on the riverbank waiting to charge at you ?

Bullrushes !

If you go to the doctor because you are a little hoarse, what is he likely to give you ?

Cough stirrup !

What do frogs do with paper ?

Rip-it !

Which dog is always making mistakes ?

A cock-up spaniel !

What is a cat's favourite TV programme ?

The Mews at Ten !

What is gray and blue and very big ?

An elephant holding it's breath !

What kind of shoes do frogs wear ?

Open-toad sandals !

Where do you find an upside-down tortoise ?

Where you left it !

Monster
Madness

Eat your sprouts, they'll put
colour in your cheeks.

But I don't want green cheeks !

What do vampires play every week ?

The National Clottery !

What should you take if a monster
invites you for dinner ?

Someone who can't run as fast as you !

Why do vampires have to
write so many letters ?

**They have to reply to their
fang clubs !**

What sort of monster wakes you up in the
morning with a nice cup of tea ?

A mummy !

Why are ghosts so bad at telling lies ?

Because you can always see through them !

The Haunted House

by

Hugo First

Mummy, what is a vampire ?

Be quiet dear and drink your blood before it clots !

What do you call an evil,
8-foot-tall, green,
hairy monster ?

Whatever he tells you to !

What is a monster's favourite handicraft ?

Tie-die !

Why didn't the witch sing at the concert ?

Because she had a frog in her throat !

What do monsters do at parties ?

They eat I-scream and jelly babies !

Did you see that wolf ?

Where ?

No, it was just an ordinary one !

Why did the young witch have such difficulty writing letters ?

She had never learnt to spell properly !

It's no good locking your door - monsters can always get in...

...They have a set of skeleton keys !

Doctor, Doctor, I have this terrible stomach ache !

**You must have eaten someone
who disagreed with you !**

A vampire's coffin fell off the back of a lorry and started rolling down a steep hill. The vampire knew exactly what to do. He went into a local chemist and asked if they had any sore throat sweets to stop his coffin !

Where do vampires keep their savings ?

In a blood bank !

What happens if you see twin witches?

You won't be able to see which witch is witch!

Why do vampires take eating so seriously ?

Because there is always so much at stake !

Where do ghosts practise frightening people ?

At boo - niversity !

What do ghosts write their letters on?

Type - frighters !

How do mummies keep a secret ?

They keep it under wraps !

What do you call a monster who never
blows his nose ?

The bogeyman !

Why do skeletons rub themselves all over with
towels when they've been swimming ?

To get bone dry !

Did you hear about the woman who wanted to marry a ghost ?

I don't know what possessed her !

A TYPICAL VAMPIRE MENU

Shepherd pie

or

Ploughman lunch

followed by

Neck-tarines with double I - scream

What's the difference between a monster and an omelette ?

One is full of yolks, the other is full of folks !

What sort of horses do monsters ride?

Night - mares !

When a monster's hungry and needs to be fed,
it's no good hiding under the bed !
He'll roll you in the mattress,
till you're buried like a mole,
then chomp you down in two big bites,
like a giant sausage roll !

Why was the monster's head sticky ?

Because he styled his hair with a honey comb !

What did the monster say when it saw someone
going past on a mountain bike ?

Yum ! Meals on wheels !

What is a vampire's favourite soup ?

Scream of mushroom !

Why don't cannibals eat weathermen?

Because they give them wind!

What's the difference between a
monster and a biscuit ?

I don't know !

Have you ever tried dunking a
monster in your tea ?

How does a vampire like his food served?

In bite-sized pieces !

A ghost went into a pub at midnight and asked the barman for a whisky. "Sorry sir," replied the barman, "we aren't allowed to serve spirits after closing time !"

PARTY GAMES FOR MONSTERS

Pass the person

Swallow the leader

What sort of monsters have wavy hair ?

Sea monsters !

What do you have to get if you invite monsters round to your house for a party ?

A new house !

Who checks the works on the ghost train ?

The ticket in - spectre !

What do Hungarian ghosts eat ?

Ghoulash !

What position does ghosts play in football teams
?

Ghoulkeepers !

How would you describe a relaxed ghost ?

Ghoul as a cucumber !

What do you call a haunted set square ?

A trian-ghoul !

What do skeletons say before eating ?

Bone appétit !

How do mummies hide ?

They wear masking tape !

Why do travelling salesmen always try to
sell things to vampires ?

Because they know they are suckers !

Where was Frankenstein's monster's head made ?

Bolton !

What did the goblin use to make himself taller ?

Elf raising flour !

What sound do baby ghosts make when they cry ?

Boo hoo !

What is the first thing a vampire sinks his fangs into after the dentist has sharpened and polished them ?

The dentist's neck !

What do ghostly boy scouts sing round the camp fire ?

Ging - gang - ghouly !

Why are ghosts no good at telling lies ?

Because you can see straight through them !

Who was James Bond's spookiest enemy ?

Ghoul - finger !

What do short-sighted ghosts wear ?

Spooktacles!

Why is Dracula so unpopular ?

Because he's a pain in the neck !

What do you do to keep ghosts fit ?

Call in an exercisist !

Knock Knock
Who's there ?
Thumping
Thumping who ?
Thumping green and scary just crawled up
your trousers !

Why don't witches ride their brooms when they're
angry?

They're afraid of flying off the handle !

Batty Brain Teasers

What do elves use to get to France ?

Cross channel fairies !

What do monsters make with cars ?

Traffic jam !

What is the name of the detective who solves all his crimes by pure accident ?

Sheer - luck Holmes !

What is the one thing you can catch with your hands tied ?

A cold !

What sort of curry do clock makers eat ?

Tikka !

Why are dentists so miserable ?

Because they are always looking down in the mouth !

Why are men with beards more honest ?

Because they can't tell bare-faced lies !

What do you get if you drop a
piano down a coal mine ?

A flat minor !

What time is it when a Chinese man visits the
dentist ?

Tooth hurty !

Which is the strongest vegetable in the garden ?

The muscle sprout !

What do sheep do on sunny days ?

Have a baa - baa - cue!

Why couldn't the squirrel building his train set ?

Because he'd eaten all the nuts !

What do you call a three legged donkey ?

A wonky !

Where did the colonel keep his armies ?

Up his sleevies !

Where would you find a rubber trumpet?

In an elastic band!

Where does tea come from?

In between the letters S and U!

What starts at the bottom and goes all the way down to the floor?

Your leg!

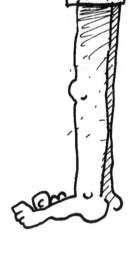

What sits in a pram and wobbles?

A jelly baby!

How do you start a teddy bear race?

Ready, teddy, go!

How do you make Scotch eggs ?

Feed your chickens whisky !

★

What gets bigger the more you take out of it ?

A hole !

How do you make a Swiss roll ?

Push him down a mountain !

*Little dog,
crossing street,
motor car,
sausage meat !*

What sort of music was invented by cavemen ?

Rock music !

What happened to the man who stole
a lorry load of prunes ?

He was on the run for months !

Waiter, there's a fly in my soup !

Thank you for telling me, sir,
I'd forgotten to put that
on the bill !

How do you get rid of a boomerang ?

Throw it down a one-way street !

What's black and white and red all over ?

A newspaper !

How does the snow queen travel about ?

On her icicle !

How do you get down from a giraffe ?

You don't get down from a giraffe - you get down from a duck !

What goes zzub, zzub ?

A bee flying backwards !

Why do cows moo ?

Because their horns don't work !

How does Dracula watch his favourite programmes ?

On a wide - scream TV !

How do you make a
Venetian blind ?

Poke him in the eyes !

What snacks do the
Russians and Americans
eat in space ?

Astronuts !

What sort of music do
miners like to listen to ?

Rock and coal !

Doctor, Doctor, I think I need glasses !

**I think you do - this isn't a doctors it's a fish
and chip shop!**

What do you call the back entrance to
a cafeteria ?

The bacteria !

What do you call
the room where
Eskimos train their
dogs ?

The mush - room !

Who swings from
cake to cake ?

Tarzipan !

Why did the doll blush ?

**Because she saw
the teddy bare !**

How do you know when it's been raining cats and dogs ?

There are lots of little poodles on the pavement !

What do you call a
cat with 8 legs ?

An octo - puss !

What do Eskimos eat for breakfast ?

Ice Crispies !

Why did the queen bee get tired of all the other bees ?

Because they kept droning on and on !

What do you get if you feed gunpowder to a chicken ?

An egg-splosion !

How do carpenters go on holiday ?

They fly there by plane !

★

Most Egyptian kings were buried with a namafor !

What's a namafor ?

Knocking nails in !

★

What do you call someone who puts bulls
to sleep ?

A bulldozer !

★

What do you call someone with jelly,
cream and fruit in their ears ?

A trifle deaf !

Crazy
Crosses

What do you get if you cross your
mum's sister with an Eskimo?

Auntie freeze!

What do you get if
you cross a
kangaroo with a
sheep?

A woolly jumper !

What do you get if
you cross a kangaroo with a line of people
waiting for a bus ?

A queue jumper !

What do you get if you cross a road without
looking ?

Run over, stupid !

What has a head and a foot but no arms ?

A bed !

★

What did one light say to the other light ?

Let's go out tonight !

What do you get if you cross an elephant with a mouse ?

Ten foot holes in your skirting board !

What do you get
if you cross
a bear with a
cow pat ?

Winnie the Pooh !

What do you get if you cross a chicken with a skunk ?

A fowl smell !

What do you get if you cross a fly with a detective ?

A police insector !

What do you call two spiders who have just got married ?

Newlywebs !

What do you get if you cross a pig with
an ambulance ?

A hambulance !

★

What do you get if you cross
a window cleaner with a giraffe ?

**A window cleaner who doesn't
need any ladders !**

★

What do you get
if you cross
a pig with Dracula
?

A hampire !

★

What do you get if you cross a chicken
with someone who tells jokes ?

A comedihen !

What do you get when you cross an elephant
with a computer ?

A lot of memory !

What do you get if you cross
a football team with ice
cream ?

Aston Vanilla !

What do you get if you
crosshockey equipment
with hiking gear ?

A pucksack !

What do you get if you cross a pig with a
mathematical quantity ?

A pork pi !

What do you get if you cross a cocker spaniel
with a poodle and a rooster ?

A cockapoodledoo!

What do you get if you cross a goldfish
bowl with a TV ?

Tele-fish-ion !

What do you get if you cross an explorer with a
cat ?

Christopher Col_umpuss !

What do you get if
you cross a
cowboy with
a dinosaur ?

Tyrannosaurus Tex !

What do you get if you cross a pudding
with an ape ?

Lemon meringue-utan !

What do you get if you cross the mafia
and a box of teaspoons ?

A gangstir !

What do you get if you cross a river with a broken bridge ?

Very wet !

What do you get if you cross a tree with a fruit ?

A pine - apple !

What do you get if you cross a math teacher with anything ?

A math teacher !

Now... TURN TO PAGE 46 OF YOUR HARD MATHS BOOK !

What do you get if you cross a chicken with a cement mixer ?

A brick layer !

What do you get if you cross a rabbit with a wolf ?

A harewolf !

What do you get if you cross a
cow pat and a microprocessor ?

A com-pooh-ter !

What do you get if you cross a mouse
and an elephant ?

An animal that's scared to look in the mirror !

What do you get
if you
cross a dog
with a worried
person ?

Nervous rex !

What do you get if you cross a duck and
a TV programme ?

A duckumentary !

What do you get if you cross rabbits
and termites ?

Bugs bunnies !

What do you get if you cross two rows of
cabbages with a main road ?

A dual cabbageway !

What do you get if
you cross kitchen
equipment with a vampire
?

Count spatula !

What do you get if you
cross a giant ape with
an aeroplane ?

King Kongcorde !

What do you get if you cross a sheep and
a porcupine ?

An animal that knits its own sweaters !

What do you get if you cross a farm worker
with some cheese and pickle ?

A ploughman's lunch !

What do you get if you cross a cat and an
octopus ?

A cat-o-nine-tails !

What do you get if you cross a
pop group with a ton of latex ?

A rubber band !

What do you get
if you cross a
cow pat with a
boomerang ?

**A nasty smell you
can't get rid of !**

What do you get if you cross dandruff
and a fried potato ?

A chip on your shoulder !

What do you get if you cross a
stick of dynamite and a pig ?

Bangers !

What do you get if you
cross a giraffe and a
cow ?

**Something you need a
ladder to milk !**

What do you get
if you cross a
traffic warden
with a dog ?

A barking ticket !

What do you get if you cross a coal mine
with a cow ?

A pit - bull !

What do you get if you cross a cow with
a CD player ?

Pop - moosic !

What do you get if you cross a pig
with a centipede ?

Bacon and legs !

What do you get if you cross a fox
with a carrot ?

**Something rabbits won't steal from the vegetable
patch !**

What do you get if you cross an outlaw with
a gift-wrapper ?

Ribbon Hood !

What Do You Call...?

What do you call a Scottish
cloak room attendant ?

Willie Angus McCoatup !

What do you call a man with a calculator on his head ?

Adam !

What do you call a cow who is a brain specialist ?

A moo - rosurgeon !

What is a rodent's favourite sport ?

Ka-rat-e !

What do you call someone with a pair of shoes on their head ?

A sole singer !

What do call a man with 6 arms ?

Andy !

What do call a man with a bowl of custard on his head ?

Spotted dick !

What do you call a fairy who never takes a bath?

Stinkerbell !

What do you call a small horse following someone ?

A pony tail !

What do you call a frog who can leave his car anywhere ?

A parking Kermit !

What do you call the college that a parrot goes to ?

A polly-technic !

What do you call a man who can sing and drink
lemonade at the same time ?

A pop singer !

What do you call a cat that is always
having accidents ?

A cat - astrophe !

What do you call a
machine for counting
cows ?

A cow - culator !

What do you call a robbery in Peking?

A Chinese take-away !

What do you call the place where sick
fairies go ?

The elf centre !

What do you call a doctor who works on the highway ?

A by-pass specialist !

What do you call the man who writes all of Dracula's jokes ?

His crypt writer !

What do you call the shark who does impersonations of one of the Beatles ?

Jaws Harrison !

What do you call work that fairies have to do after school ?

Gnomework !

What do you call a streetlight where monsters hang around waiting for victims ?

A ghoulpost !

What do you call the carpet cleaner that vampires use ?

A victim cleaner !

What do you call it when your teacher is having a baby ?

A Miss-conception !

What do you call a spanner belonging to a toad ?

A toad's tool !

What do you call a feline fashion show ?

A cat - walk !

What do you call a dead parrot ?

A polygon !

What do you call a dinosaur that smashes everything in it's path ?

Tyrranosaurus Wrecks !

What do you call someone who doesn't use a handkerchief ?

Greensleeves !

What do you call a prisoner's pet budgie ?

A jailbird !

What do you call it when someone tries to rob a bank with a bunch of flowers ?

A violet robbery !

What do you call the largest mouse in the World ?

Hippopotamouse !

What do you call it when you pick up the phone and send elephants charging in the opposite direction ?

A reverse-charge call !

What do you call a Teddy bear's favourite drink ?

Ginger bear !

What do you call the skeleton who was once the Emperor of France ?

Napoleon Boney Parts !

What do you call a cat that works in a hospital ?

A first aid kitty !

What do you call a cat that plays the drums ?

A drum kitty !

What do you call a cat that makes models ?

A construction kitty !

What do you call a country where everyone has to drive a red automobile ?

A red carnation !

What do you call the last man to abandon ship ?

Deaf !

What do you call the Elizabethan explorer who cold stop bicycles ?

Sir Francis Brake !

What do you call the explorer who was caught and eaten by cannibals ?

Captain Cooked !

What do you call a man with a toilet on his head ?

Lou !

(Of course, he might have two if he was feeling flush !)

What do you call a boomerang that doesn't work ?

A stick !

What do you call a cat in a panic ?

Cat flap !

What do you call the biggest ant in the World ?

An eleph - ant !

What do you call a house where Martians live ?

A greenhouse !

What do you call 20 rabbits moving backwards ?

A receding hare line !

What do you call a dog that likes doing experiments ?

A Lab-rador !

What do you call chees that isn't yours ?

Nacho cheese !

What do you call the dance where all cakes are invited ?

A-bun-dance !

What do you call it when two cows munch grass side by side to keep warm ?

Double grazing !

What do you call a sheep dog when
it has eaten too much melon ?

Melancholy !

What do you call a highly dangerous cake ?

Atilla the Bun !

What do you call the cake that was served after
the battle of the Little Big Horn ?

Custer's Slices !

What do you call a cake you can use to
power your portable CD ?

Current cake !

What do you call a cake you can give to mice ?

Cheesecake !

What do you call a cake you eat in the bath?

Sponge!

What do you call a dog that likes wrapping presents?

A boxer!

What do you Santa's helpers?

Subordinate clauses!

What do you call a man with no shins?

Tony!

What do you call a chimney built upside down?

A well!

What do you call a nervous witch?

A twitch!

What do you call the pliers you use in
math class?

Multipliers !

What do you call small change that can't go to
the toilet ?

Coin-stipated !

What do you call stupid flowers that grow
in a pond ?

Water sillies !

What do you call a sheep with fangs ?

A lamb-pire !

What do you call a Shakespearian actor
who eats garlic ?

Macbreath !

Mirthful
Miscellany

Did you hear about the girl who
fell asleep with her head
under the pillow ?

The fairies came and
took out all her teeth !

Where has all the lemonade gone. I though we
agreed to have half the bottle each ?

**We did – my half was the bottom half, so I had
to drink yours to get to it !**

Fish and chips and mushy peas ? But I ordered
a ploughman's lunch !

**That's what then ploughman is having for his
lunch today !**

Doctor, doctor, my little boy has swallowed all
the coins from my purse !

**Don't worry – the change will probably do him
good !**

Dad, am I worth a million pounds to you ?

Of course you are, son !

**In that case can you lend me some of it now,
I want to go out tonight !**

What did the lovesick bull say to the cow?

'When I fall in love it will be for heifer !'

What do you get if you dial 666 ?

Three policemen standing on their heads !

Where does the local policeman live ?

At 999, Letsby Avenue !

Why was the policeman offered a job
on the buses ?

Because copper is such a good conductor !

What do you call a sheep with no legs
or head ?

A cloud !

Did you hear about the policeman who
was invited to join the theatre ?

He always gave an arresting performance !

What does a policeman call an overdue library fine ?

An old bill !

What goes 'ello, ello, tick, tock,
woof, ello, ello, tick, tock, woof' ?

A police watchdog !

What goes 'ho, ho, ho, ho, clonk' ?

Someone laughing their head off !

Why do witches fly around on broomsticks ?

**Because vacuum cleaners don't have long
enough cables !**

What did the policeman say to his tummy ?

I've got you under a vest !

★

What do you do if your nose goes on strike ?

Picket !

★

What tables can't
you eat ?

Vegetables !

★

Why do bicycles
never do anything
exciting ?

**Because they are
always two-tyred !**

★

What is the easiest way to count a herd
of cattle?

Use a cowculator!

What comes after the letter A ?

The rest of the alphabet !

Why didn't the Roman chicken cross the road?

Because she was afraid someone would caesar!

I would tell you the joke about the bed...

...but it hasn't been made yet !

What's red on the outside and grey and crowded on the inside ?

A bus full of elephants !

What does an elephant do when it rains ?

It gets wet !

How do you stop your dog barking in the back of the car ?

Put it in the front !

What is worse than finding a maggot when you bite into an apple ?

Finding half a maggot !

What is brown and sticky ?

A stick !

What is green and bouncy ?

A spring onion !

Why do wizards drink so much tea ?

Because sorcerers need cuppas !

How do you cut through the waves ?

With a sea-saw !

What sort of nuts
sneeze the most ?

Cashews !

What exams are
horses good at ?

Hay levels !

Why did the owl
make everyone
laugh ?

**Because he was a
hoot !**

If your cat ate a lemon what would
he become ?

A sourpuss !

Will you remember me tomorrow ?

Yes !

Will you remember me next week ?

Yes !

Will you remember me next month ?

Yes !

Will you remember me in a year ?

Yes !

Knock, knock

Who's there ?

You see, you've forgotten me already !

Knock Knock...
Who's there ?
Ivor...
Ivor who ?
**Ivor good mind not
to tell you !**

What do you give a sick elephant ?

**Plenty of room !
Knock Knock...**

Who's there ?
Justin...
Justin who ?
Justin time for a party !

How can you tell if there's
an elephant in your school
custard ?

It's lumpier than usual !

What is the difference between a jeweller
and a prison warden ?

One sells watches the other watches cells !

Which is the strongest day of the week ?

**Sunday - because all the others are weak
days !**

Why didn't the viper viper nose ?

Because the adder adder handkerchief !

What's the difference between a fisherman
and a lazyschoolboy ?

**One baits hooks, the other
hates books !**

Why did the jam roll ?

**Because it saw the
apple turnover !**

Two cows were
talking in a field...

First cow - Are you
worried about this
mad cow disease ?

Second cow - Why
should I worry about
that - I'm a penguin !

What do you get if you cross a snowman and a
mosquito ?

Frostbite !

What zooms along the bed of the lake ?

A motor pike and side carp !

Why shouldn't you complain about
the price of a train ticket ?

Because it's bound to be fare !

How do you tell which end
of a worm is the head ?

**Tickle it in the middle and see
which end laughs !**

Romeo - Do you love me ?

Juliet - Of course I do !

Romeo - Then whisper something soft and
sweet !

Juliet - Lemon meringue pie !

Angry old man - I'll teach you to throw stones at my greenhouse !

Naughty boy - I wish you would, I keep missing !

Did you hear about the man who was hit on the head with a pan full of curry ?

He ended up in a korma !

Where do cows go on Saturday night ?

To the moo - vies !

What happens when pigs fly ?

The price of bacon goes up !

Why did the tap dancer have to retire ?

He kept falling into the sink !

What is the difference between a nail
and a bad boxer ?

**One gets knocked in, the other gets
knocked out !**

What do you call the story of The
Three Little Pigs ?

A pigtail !

How does a chimpanzee make toast ?

Puts it under a gorilla !

What do jelly babies
wear in the rain ?

Gum boots !

What is small, green
and goes camping ?

A boy sprout !

What does a Swedish Fred Flintstone shout?

Abba dabba Doo!

What do you get when you cross a jelly with a sheep dog?

Collie wobbles!

What kind of ears does a train have?

Engineers!

Why was the farmer hopping mad?

Because someone trod on his corn!

A neutron goes into a bar and asks the bartender, "How much for a beer?" The bartender replies, "For you, no charge."

Why is a farmer cruel ?

Because he pulls corn by its ears !

How do you use an
Egyptian Mummy's
doorbell ?

Toot-and-come-in !

Why couldn't the
butterfly get into
the dance ?

**Because it was a
moth-ball !**

Why did the orange stop halfway up the hill ?

Because it ran out of juice !

Joe - Mum, do you notice any change in me ?

Mum - No, why do you ask ?

Joe - Because I've just swallowed 5p !

How do you know when there's an elephant
hiding under your bed ?

Your nose touches the ceiling !

Waiter, waiter, what do you call this ?

It's bean soup sir !

I don't care what it's been - what is it now ?

I would tell you the joke about the butter - but
you would only spread it !

And - I would tell
you the joke about
the fence - but I
know you would
never get over it !

Did you hear about the new restaurant they
built on the Moon ?

The food is great but it has no atmosphere !

Who makes a fish's dreams come true ?

The fairy cod-mother !

What shoot along the washing line at
70 miles an hour?

Hondapants !

How can you keep cool at a football match ?

Stand next to a fan !

What do you get if you
cross a crocodile with
a rose ?

**I don't know but I
wouldn't try smelling it !**

Who did Dracula marry ?

The girl necks door !

Did you hear about the two flies playing football in the saucer – they were practising for the cup !

What did the baby chicken say when his *mum* laid a jar of orange jam ?

Ooh ! Look what marma-lade !

Why wouldn't the hot dog star in the movies ?

Because the rolls weren't good enough !

How do you keep an idiot in suspense ?

I'll tell you tomorrow !

Where do monsters stay on holiday ?

In a bed-for-breakfast hotel !

What is black and white and pink all over ?

An embarrassed zebra !

What sort of car does a farmer's dog drive ?

A Range Rover !

Did you hear about
the burglar who was
arrested in his shower
- he was trying to
make a clean getaway !

How do you make a
band stand ?

Hide all their chairs !

Policeman - You just went through a red light !

**Motorist - Sorry, blame it on my good manners.
My mum taught me never to look when someone
was changing !**

And always remember that before you give someone a piece of your mind, make sure you can manage on what you have left !

What sort of shoes can you make from banana skins ?

Slippers !

Jim- My sister married an Irishman !

Joe - Oh. Really ?

Jim - No, O'Reilly !

Woodwork teacher - What are you making ?

Pupil - A portable.

Woodwork teacher - A portable what ?

Pupil - I don't know yet - I only just made the handle !

Mum - Why haven't you changed the water in the goldfish bowl ?

Daughter - Because they haven't drunk the first lot yet !

What do you do with a sick budgie ?

Send it for tweetment !

Who makes suits and eats spinach?

Popeye the Tailorman !

Are those bongos dangling from your ears ?

No, they're my ear drums !

Did you hear about the man who went to the doctor and told him he thought he was a suitcase ?

The doctor sent him packing !

Have you heard about the magic tractor?

It turned into a field !